## THE WEEKEND DECORATOR
# BACKGROUNDS AND BORDERS

THE WEEKEND DECORATOR

# BACKGROUNDS AND BORDERS

## PAMELA INNES
### WORKPAPER DESIGNS BY SARA JOHN

AURUM PRESS

# For Matthew and Diana

ACKNOWLEDGEMENTS

The author and publisher would like to thank the following for their help in the creation of this book: Robert Lillis and B&Q in Bristol; Juliet Bawden, Sarah Curren, Cookie Galloway and Brats Ltd. in London.

## A NOTE ON QUANTITIES

Paint quantities are given in millilitres, litres and grammes (for powder paints). Approximate conversion to U.S. measurements are as follows:

100 ml = $3\frac{1}{2}$ fluid ounces
1 litre = $1\frac{3}{4}$ pints
5 litres = 1 gallon
100 grams = 4 ounces

First published 1996 by Aurum Press Limited,
25 Bedford Avenue, London WC1B 3AT

Copyright © 1996 by Pamela Innes

A catalogue record of this book is available from the British Library.

ISBN 1 85410 428 4

Graphics and workpapers by Sara John
Photography by Marie-Louise Avery and Jonathan Metcalf
Styling by Margaret Caselton
Edited by Judy Spours
Designed by Donald Macpherson

Printed in Singapore by Imago

# CONTENTS

# INTRODUCTION

Five years ago I moved from a very grand townhouse in The Hague in the Netherlands to a modest Victorian terraced house in the centre of Bristol, England. Although the two houses differed greatly in atmosphere and character, they had one thing in common: both were the victims of enthusiastic but somewhat misplaced decorating zeal.

The Hague house had once belonged to an equerry of the former queen, Juliana, and had six bathrooms and a marble entrance hall. The sheer size and height of the rooms regularly dismayed old friends in ancient cardigans who had simply dropped in for a game of Scrabble. This old mansion had been decorated within an inch of its elegant life by the previous chatelaine, a volatile Frenchwoman of indefatigable energy whose life's work had been to restore and 'knock it into shape'. She had spent twelve years remodelling the old place. Rich wallpapers had been applied to newly-plastered walls and pristine parquet covered the old floorboards. (She had even had the floorboards lifted and vacuumed underneath.) In the power struggle between mere mortal and bricks and mortar, this feisty Frenchwoman had undoubtedly won, and the old house stood stiffly and rather uneasily to attention, wondering where next its private parts were to be exposed and assailed with a vacuum cleaner.

I found the modest house in Bristol on a wet morning in May, lurking behind a cinema. It was a friendly place, and welcoming. Its proud owner had not gone as far as vacuuming the joists, but he had covered every inch of original floorboard and tesselated floor tile with close carpeting or fuzzy brown carpet squares. Unsightly cracks in the plaster were cunningly concealed behind meticulous Regency stripes, and the ornamental plaster architraves had been carefully filled in with crisp white paint. The house drooped beneath the weight of brass chandeliers suspended from low ceilings and quietly grieved for the old, pre-DIY days of plain and painted walls, when a maid with a speaking tube next to her bed slept in the small top room.

The desire to furnish and decorate domestic interiors is as old as time itself. In ancient Pompeii, for instance, houses were built with rooms facing inwards away from the road, and, perhaps to compensate for the lack of a view, their owners enriched the walls with murals of gods and heroes, soaring columns and fantastic architecture. Some of the earliest illustrations of domestic interiors are found in Renaissance paintings. Carpaccio's 'Nativity of the Virgin', dating from the end of the fifteenth century, gives priority to the room the Virgin occupies rather than the Biblical story itself. There are gaily chequered tiles on the floor and the bed-covers and curtains are brightly patterned. Pewter mugs and candlesticks are arranged on a shelf, and there is a wonderfully ornate rug draped over a wooden settle, drawn conversationally close to the bed. The inhabitants of this house clearly cared about its ambience. There is an integrity and harmony about the room which inspired Carpaccio, and he used it to underline his message about the holy mother and child

Up to the present century, it was primarily the architect who had control over the total design of a house, from the external structure to the smallest details in a finished room, the light fittings and door knobs. He even designed the furniture to complement the scheme and produce a unified work of art. Mass-production shifted the balance and the brilliant architect-designer, with his team of creative craftsmen – wood-carvers, marblers, gilders and furniture-makers – began to be eclipsed. In their place came an increasing number of ordinary people who were prepared and confident enough to decide for themselves the way in which their homes would be arranged.

Although a desire for decoration is natural, it is sometimes easy to forget the need to decorate wisely and well. In the near-panic to get it all done, it is easy to overlook that there are rules to be followed in the applied arts just as there are in fine art painting. The most basic law is an understanding of the underlying structure of the house to be decorated, which is particularly apposite to the decoration of walls. I took my Bristol house at its own pace, and tried to keep its particular character firmly in mind.

It is wise to do this even when gripped by the decorating excitement which has taken hold in recent years. Decorating books have made ragging, dragging, sponging and the like available to DIY painters, and it is no surprise that they have thrown themselves on pale emulsioned walls with rags, brushes and great glee. The new effects added colour and interest to magnolia lives, and busy rag-rolling, over-kill stencils and elaborate window treatments became a feature of many homes. 'First take your scumble...', rather like Mrs Beeton's recipe instruction 'First take twelve chickens...', became the passwords for home decorators, irrespective of the size and character of their homes.

For the most part, untrained and unskilled DIY people are equipped only with huge enthusiasm and energy. They have a great need to adapt the pre-existing shell they have moved into to

suit their own needs and lifestyle as far as their imaginations and resources allow. They have an unprecedented interest in the way their homes are decorated, and many use museums and stately homes, as well as magazines and books, as reference sources for ideas – gaining in the process a great sense of colour and history.

This book is to provide advice for such home decorators on painting walls. It tackles such problems as how to control the colour on large areas of wall which can easily overpower everything else; how to deal with the mess and disruption that DIY can cause. It is for people who happily combine interesting, sometimes brilliant colours for their wardrobe but who go to pieces when confronted with a wall which needs a lick of paint. Until recently, painting a room was a serious, sometimes dreaded activity involving dust-sheets, furniture removal and careful planning. The new approach to decorating is freer, more creative and, using simple and sometimes unorthodox materials, much more fun.

The background colours and textures of the walls themselves are our starting-point, the primed canvas onto which the more creative elements of decorating can be applied. The book also looks at painted and stencilled borders, cunningly devised frescoes, painting on tiles and on fabric wall-hangings, and extending the decorative feel of a room to built-in furniture. It shows how decoration can enhance the overall feel and furnishings of your home, rather than compete with them.

Dictators, kings, scientists, poets and bankers have all, at one time or another, escaped the pressures and mundanity of their daily lives and used their homes to indulge a deep-rooted artistic instinct. Someone once said 'an apartment is a mood'. This is a sentiment understood by anyone who has painted a new colour onto the walls of a home. The place we live in, however modest, is our own blank canvas where we can freely express the need for decoration that is within us all.

# SETTING THE SCENE WITH COLOUR

The decision about which colour to paint the walls is the biggest and most crucial for home decorators faced with a room which needs improvement. Walls play such a prominent part in the scheme of things: they are the background to the design picture, the framework for furniture and accessories. It is the colour treatment of the large surface area of the walls which sets the mood for the rest of the room and which can make or break a whole scheme.

Many interior designers suggest that a board pasted up with fabric scraps and paint colours is an essential aid when considering the colour scheme of a room. I have found that although they are some help in planning an overall strategy, the samples are so small that the colours are difficult to 'translate' visually to huge areas of wall. I am inclined to bite the bullet and paint out all walls with a flat, off-white paint. Just living with this soothing neutral for a few days gives a much better idea of a room's shape and proportions. You can also clearly see the way natural light and electric light work at specific times of the day.

At this point I usually pour a drink and think about the colour. Take a long, hard look at your newly-painted walls and picture your favourite shade, one which will match or tone with the next largest expanse of colour in the room – probably the carpet, sofa or curtains. A paler shade of this predominant colour, mixed to a glaze and softly blended over the flat paint, will texture the walls in such a way that they look dappled with light. Using a brush, sponge, or even an old cloth, and allowing the background neutral to glimmer through, the walls will immediately begin to look richer, more alive – designed.

I have deliberately chosen deep, strong shades for the first two-tone sponged effect to demonstrate just how subtle a background can be, even when using strong colour tones. It is the application of a softening glaze which makes it possible to achieve depth and drama and still retain an unintrusive background to blend with existing furnishings.

Hallways are often a problem in houses of whatever age or size. The first instinct is to slap on as much white paint as possible, but this will rarely increase the feeling of light and space, as the pale paint tends to emphasize the walls, thus making the space seem even more confined. The trick is to 'lose' the walls and open them up with a broken paint effect. An easy technique is to use two pale, home-made glazes sponged on in a marbled effect which leaves the base coat shimmering through.

# AN AUTUMN GOLD STUDY

## SHOPPING LIST

(For an average size room,
approximately 12 x 12 feet, 16 square metres.)

5 litre tin of warm pinky-red vinyl matt emulsion
Large decorating brush
Half-litre tawny red vinyl matt emulsion
Half-litre tin golden yellow vinyl matt emulsion
200 ml bottle glycerine
Two natural sea sponges
Litre matt acrylic varnish
Varnishing brush or fine-bristle decorating brush

# AN AUTUMN GOLD STUDY
## Step-by-step
### Painting and sponging in strong colours

### 1.

If walls are in poor condition, see page 74. If walls are in reasonable condition, sand smooth any bumps or flaking paint and wash down with household detergent or sugar soap. Be sure to remove all traces of the cleaner with a thorough rinse and allow to dry completely.

### 2.

Paint the wall with a base of warm pinky-red. Allow to dry and apply a second coat to cover smoothly.

### 3.

While the paint is drying, mix two glazes, one tinted with tawny red emulsion, the other with golden yellow emulsion. These are made by diluting the half-litre of emulsion with 150 ml water, then mixing in three tablespoons of glycerine. The glycerine helps the paint to flow on more smoothly and keep the edges wet while working.

*Applying the base colour with a paintbrush.*

*Sponging on the first glaze, tawny red.*

### 4.

Pick up the tawny red glaze in a damp sea sponge and apply to the wall using firm, 'pecking' movements. Leave plenty of background colour showing through. Work in areas of approximately one square metre, moving diagonally across the wall from top to bottom and leaving an uneven edge for the next application to slot into seamlessly.

### 5.

While the paint is still wet, soften the hard outlines with a clean, damp sponge. Work from the middle of the sponged areas, softening and blending, out towards the edges so that they merge with the background colour. Allow to dry.

### 6.

Using a clean, damp sea sponge, apply the golden yellow glaze randomly across and around the softened tawny red areas so that the two colours dapple and merge into each other.

*Softening harsh outlines with a damp sponge.*

*Sponging on a second colour, golden yellow.*

# AN AUTUMN GOLD STUDY
## *Step-by-step*

### 7.

Whilst still damp, and with a clean damp sponge, once more blend any remaining hard edges, working both glazes together to give a soft, marbled effect. Allow to dry completely and finish with two coats of matt acrylic varnish.

*Softening and blending both colours with a damp sponge.*

# A BLUE SKY HALLWAY

# A BLUE SKY HALLWAY
*Step-by-step*
*Sponging with home-made glazes*

**1.**

Apply two smooth coats of magnolia vinyl silk emulsion to the prepared walls and allow to dry. Mix tinted glazes of sky blue and rich beige as described for the previous project (*see* page 14).

**2.**

With a damp sea sponge, apply random patterns of the sky blue glaze, allowing plenty of the base-coat magnolia to show through. Work in areas of about a square metre diagonally across the wall, keeping the edges wet to ensure that the next area sponged joins imperceptibly.

**3.**

While still damp and with a clean, damp sea sponge, soften any hard edges and sponge impressions, pushing and blending the blue glaze into the background colour.

**4.**

While the paint is still damp, apply the rich beige glaze with a sponge, working both around and across the sky blue areas, and blending both into the background magnolia colour.

*Applying sky blue glaze with a damp sponge.*

*Sponging on the second, rich beige glaze.*

**5.**

Soften all hard edges with a damp sponge, further blending together so that the glazes and background marble softly together.

**6.**

When dry, dilute a small amount of magnolia with 30 per cent water. Soften around the the edges of the coloured glazes, again using a sponge, merging any remaining areas of dark colour. Allow to dry.

**7.**

Paint the walls with a coat of matt acrylic varnish.

*Softening with sponge and diluted magnolia emulsion.*

# A DOVE GREY BEDROOM

Our bedroom demonstrates a cool colour scheme for those whose appetite for the visual image has already been sated by the bustle of daily life. Using a technique borrowed from the Scandinavians, who are experts in the use of all shades of pale, we used grey and off-white to create an unintrusive atmosphere where you can escape to relax and think. Pale serenity is a Scandinavian art form.

Such muted tones can also be used on the walls of a room where the objects you wish to display are more important than the room itself. If you have bright, modern paintings or a lively, patterned rug which you want to show off, you will need the subtlest of backgrounds against which to display them to best advantage. Our pale emulsion, roughly brushed over with grey glaze, provides the perfect cool, textured environment to act as a backdrop.

The bedroom we worked on was a simple, square boxroom with no redeeming features, so we added blown-vinyl borders above the skirting, lightly dusted with powdered graphite, to add weight and visual interest to the scheme. Many people use borders as a quick way to add a little interest to an otherwise dull room, in the form of jaunty chains of flowers and bows in procession around doors and over windows. These tend to look frivolous and can often be irrelevant to the overall scheme. Textured borders work better, and can be incorporated into the colour scheme of the whole room.

In the eighteenth century, *papier mâché* or 'composition' wall decorations – a mixture of resin, glue and whiting – were suggested by architect Robert Adam as a cheap alternative to expensive carved wood. His idea only came to fruition in the late nineteenth century, when cast plastic was mass-produced in the form of lincrusta and linoleum.

Its refined, twentieth-century form is vinyl, 'blown' to produce a raised, patterned effect. Many contemporary designs are over elaborate, but the clean and classic versions now also available are something different, acceptable even to the most refined tastes. Such blown vinyl papers and borders provide a wonderful, inexpensive source of texture for walls, even in modern houses, and they are very easy to apply and decorate. The newest are based on Robert Adam's own designs, architectural in atmosphere and very elegant, and can lift a room into quite another style.

# A COOL ROOM

## SHOPPING LIST

(For a room approximately 12 x 12 feet – 16 square metres.)

5 litre tin dove white vinyl matt emulsion
Large decorating brush
Litre of silver-grey vinyl matt emulsion
200 ml bottle of glycerine
Paint kettle or cleaned, empty paint tin to hold 2 litres

# A COOL ROOM
## *Step-by-step*
## *Colourbrushing*

### 1.

Base-coat the prepared wall with dove white emulsion. Allow to dry and sand lightly. If necessary, paint on a second, dense, smooth coat. Allow to dry.

### 2.

Dilute the silver-grey emulsion with a quarter of a litre of water and mix thoroughly. Add four tablespoons of glycerine and mix again.

### 3.

Using the large decorating brush, apply the silver-grey glaze to the wall with broad, sweeping strokes. Leave plenty of the background colour shimmering through, and criss-cross the brushstrokes across the wall. The aim is to leave subtle brushmarks. There is no need to soften them as they will blend into the background as the glaze dries.

*Diluting dove grey emulsion with glycerine.*

*Applying glaze with brush in criss-cross effect.*

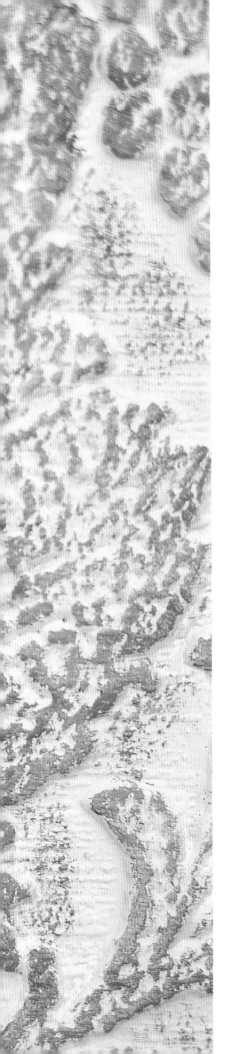

# A BLOWN VINYL BORDER

## SHOPPING LIST

(For a room approximately 12 x 12 feet – 16 square metres.)

Blown vinyl wallpaper or borders
All purpose wallpaper paste
Litre dove white vinyl matt emulsion
1½-inch all-purpose decorating brush
Small tin powdered graphite (available from art
and craft shops)
Soft, lint-free cloths

# A BLOWN VINYL BORDER
*Step-by-step*
*Powdered graphite on textured paper*

### 1.

Mix the wallpaper paste thickly, according to the packet instructions for heavy papers. Paste the border to the prepared and painted wall, lining up the pattern at corners, cutting where necessary.

### 2.

With the decorating brush, paint on two coats of dove white emulsion, working the paint thoroughly into the raised pattern.

### 3.

When the paint is thoroughly dry, pour the powdered graphite into a saucer, then pick up with a clean, damp cloth, blowing off any loose, excess particles. Gently rub the graphite across the raised areas of the border, using a circular movement. It is best to start with a small amount of graphite and a light application until you see the finished effect. Depth of colour can be gradually built up.

*Pasting the border to the wall.*

*Painting border with dove grey emulsion.*

### 4.

If the powder has gone on too heavily in some areas, stipple paint over it using the dove white, then re-graphite lightly when dry. Unless the walls are to have a great deal of wear and tear, there is no need to varnish them.

*Using a cloth to rub graphite over raised areas of the border.*

# A BURNISHED ROMAN BATHROOM

The bathroom can be a cold and clinical room, so we decided to transform ours into a warm, inviting place to take a bath - even with an added hint of Roman decadence. The walls are burnished bronze using a technique of coloured powders gently polished on with acrylic scumble, a transparent glaze into which colours are mixed to produce a soft effect. This gives a richness and depth to strong tones which avoids the flat colours becoming overpowering. Anyone who has lovingly polished a piece of furniture can handle this technique, which incidentally allows you to dictate precisely the depth of colour you want by the amount of powder you apply.

We then employed a new *découpage* technique in imitation of a Pompeiian fresco. Many actual frescoes survived and were revealed by the eighteenth-century excavation of Pompeii from the preserving lava of Mount Vesuvius, which had erupted on the city in the first century AD. The Pompeiians lived in a world of make-believe when they were at home, a *trompe l'oeil* universe where surrounding walls were decorated with fantasy columns and architecture, views of sea, sky and gardens, inhabited by gods, heroes and animals – sometimes even life-size portraits of their family. This was their antidote to urban living of the first century.

Inspired by this concept, I searched history books for elevating subjects to paint on the wall. Gods and heroes might be a little hard to compete with first thing in the morning, but I found a charming mosaic of doves drinking from a basin which I thought would be a soothing subject to contemplate at any time of day, and which I could reproduce simply and easily using a colour photocopier.

To complement further the deep, rich environment of the new bathroom, I decided to paint the tiles to imitate a rich marble. Existing tiles are difficult to remove and expensive to replace, and it is therefore often much better to paint them. Many people hesitate to do this because of a misguided feeling that the tiles are an integral part of the building, or because of an underlying doubt that paint can stick and remain waterproof on such impervious, shiny surfaces. Paint manufacturers are now producing products designed to form a second skin over most surfaces, and if properly applied are extremely durable. We transformed our cheap white tiles into very expensive looking slate coloured marble with the minimum of cost or effort. The whole room is now one to spend time in and to relax in.

# BURNISHED BATHROOM WALLS

# BURNISHED BATHROOM WALLS
### *Step-by-step*
### *Powder pigmenting walls*

### 1.

The technique works best on a rough surface, so there is no need to sand down the walls. Apply two coats of barley white emulsion and allow to dry.

### 2.

Transfer the acrylic scumble glaze to a plate or saucer. On a white dinner plate, make three separate piles of the powder colours.

### 3.

Bunch up a damp absorbent cotton cloth in the hand and dip it into the scumble glaze. Pick up some yellow powder and apply to the wall, rubbing gently with a circular movement until all the powder has been worked in. Start at the top of the wall and work diagonally across and down, avoiding straight lines, which may remain visible.

### 4.

Alternately picking up scumble glaze and the three shades of powder, cover the wall in light and dark tones of colour, polishing them in gently with the cloth. The Sienna yellow should predominate, with softer highlights of red and ochre.

### 5.

When dry, paint over the walls with matt acrylic varnish.

*Applying powder to the wall using a damp cloth.*

# A POMPEIIAN FRESCO

# A POMPEIIAN FRESCO
### *Step-by-step*
### *The new* découpage

### 1.

Roughly tear the fresco illustration around the edges, making one or two fairly deep V-shapes into the picture. Tearing from the back will avoid the white reverse-side edge showing. When stuck onto the wall, the illustration will look worn with age.

### 2.

Stick the torn illustration to the wall with wallpaper paste, finishing with a coat over the top. Make sure that all the torn edges are firmly stuck down. Clean off any excess paste with a clean, damp cloth and allow to dry.

*Tearing the photocopy around the edges.*

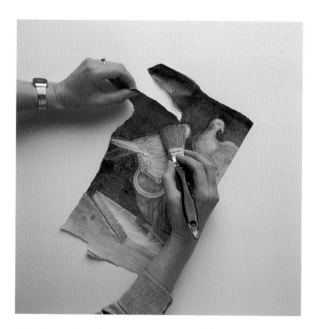

*Pasting the photocopy to a wall.*

### 3.

Pour the acrylic scumble glaze into a container and the powder pigment onto a plate. With a damp cotton cloth, pick up the scumble glaze and then the yellow powder. Gently polish the surface of the illustration, using a circular motion. The pigment will 'age' the new colours of the illustration.

### 4.

When dry, paint over with matt acrylic varnish.

*Using cloth to apply pigments to the photocopy to 'age' it.*

# RICH MARBLED TILES

# RICH MARBLED TILES
## *Step-by-step*
## *Marbling tiles*

### 1.

Rub over the surface of the tiles with wire-wool to roughen, and with a wet brush paint on a smooth, thin coat of tile primer to completely cover. Allow to dry.

### 2.

Paint the tiles with a base of mid-olive green. Allow to dry and lightly sand with fine-grade sandpaper. Paint with a second coat, working the paint into the grout lines between the tiles. Allow to dry.

*Painting tiles with mid-olive green base coat.*

### 3.

Place the scumble glaze in a container and the powder pigments on a large plate. With a damp stippling brush, pick up the scumble glaze and then the individual powders onto the tips of the bristles. Stipple onto the tiles with a firm 'pouncing' movement, holding the brush almost at right angles and blending the colours together. Create small areas of colour, leaving plenty of the background showing through.

*Stippling powder paints onto the tiles.*

### 4.

With a clean brush, work the powders into the background, softening along any hard edges of colour. Aim for a marbled effect, with the powder colour dappling into the background.

### 5.

When completely dry, varnish with at least two coats of matt polyurethane varnish.

*Using the stippling brush to blend the powder colours together.*

*Varnishing the tiles.*

 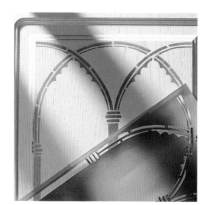 

# APPLIED DECORATION

When a pre-historic artist first daubed earth colour around the outstretched fingers of his left hand, making a living stencil, he created an interior design idea which has persisted ever since. His stencilled design is still on the walls of a cave in Lascaux in France, and our enthusiasm for this simplest of paint techniques remains. The enduring charm of stencilling must be that it is so easy to do. With the design safely captured on card we are free to indulge our creative talent and concentrate on the arrangement and colouring of the pattern. Stencilling makes artists of us all.

Stencils enjoyed a particular popularity in the late 1970s, although the barrage of bows and festoon flowers were not to the liking of those who prefer a streamlined interior. But now new geometrical and architectural stencil designs are available to complement a taste for less fussy interiors, and stencilling is an art form which continues to thrive.

I have included three stencil ideas in this book, all uncomplicated and classic, suitable for modern or older houses. The first stencil design has been applied to an otherwise very conventional wardrobe. Flat-pack furniture for building into a room is a sturdy and affordable answer to the problem of storage in smaller houses, yet it is almost always bland and soulless. The stencil I have designed is deliberately architectural to enhance the look of a large wardrobe, and has Gothic overtones, alluding to the designs favoured by British designers at the turn of the nineteenth and twentieth centuries. It is a very quick solution to blank cupboard doors, especially if you use spray paint, and the idea can be extended to decorate matching curtain fabric.

The stencil which surrounds the bathroom fresco (*see* page 55) can also be used as a continuous run in any room. As a border to the fresco, it is faded into the polished powder background, with parts deliberately missed out as though they had worn away.

The other stencil is a simple border design to improve the proportions of the sort of slim, plain door-frames which are now built into new houses. A stencil around a doorway is a nifty way of linking two colour schemes in adjacent rooms – a pale hallway leading into a darker sitting-room, perhaps, or an *en suite* bathroom off a bedroom. Using the leftover paint from both to colour the stencil around the doorway, the scheme looks planned, the two rooms linked.

# A TRACERY WARDROBE

## SHOPPING LIST

Workpaper Design A1 and Design A2
Oiled stencil card
Sharp scalpel or small, pointed scissors
Transfer or carbon paper
HB pencil
Long ruler
Tin of spray mount
Tin willow green decorative spray paint
White spirit
Newspapers
Face mask and rubber gloves
Masking tape

# A TRACERY WARDROBE
## *Step-by-step*
## *Stencilling on furniture and fabric*

### *1.*

Transfer the designs of Workpapers A1 (door stencil) and A2 (curtain stencil) onto stencil card (*see* page 78). Extend the stencil where indicated to make pillars which fit the length of your doors. Include 'bridges' (*see* page 80) to keep the lengthened pillars stable.

### *2.*

Spray mount the back of the stencil card A1 and stick it firmly to the area of the door to be stencilled.

### *3.*

Cover all areas adjacent to the stencil with newspapers, including the floor. Open all windows and wear face mask and gloves.

### *4.*

Shake the spray paint can thoroughly and after a trial squirt onto newspaper to get the paint flowing smoothly, spray through the stencil design with smooth, short bursts.

*Spray mounting the stencil to the surface of the wardrobe.*

*After masking the surrounding area, testing the spray paint on newspaper.*

### 5.

When dry, remove stencil, and if necessary clean off any smudges with white spirit and a soft cloth.

### 6.

Cut curtain fabric to the required size and mark out hems and seams with a 2B pencil. Measure out and mark where stencil design A2 will be applied.

### 7.

Prepare a thick layer of newspaper flat on a table, lay on the curtain fabric and fix it with masking tape.

*Applying the spray paint to the stencil.*

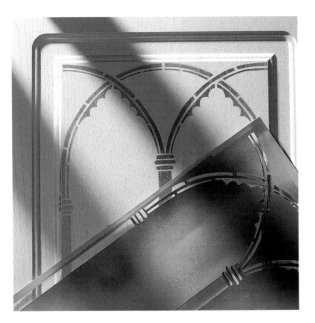

*Removing the stencil card to reveal the design.*

*Masking off the fabric surrounding the curtain stencil.*

# A TRACERY WARDROBE
## *Step-by-step*

**8.**

Spray mount the back of stencil A2 and stick it firmly to the fabric.

**9.**

Hold the can approximately nine inches from the surface of the fabric and spray the paint over with short, smooth bursts. Move the stencil and newspaper to the next area to be painted and repeat until the fabric is covered with the design.

*Revealing the stencilled material.*

# BATHROOM
# FRESCO STENCIL

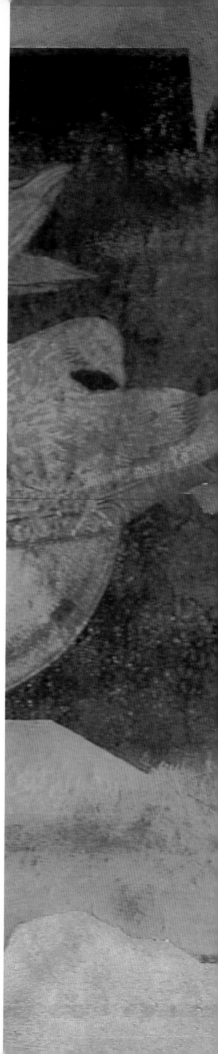

## SHOPPING LIST

Work paper Design B
HB pencil
Transfer or carbon paper
Scalpel or small sharp scissors
Stippling or stencil brush
75g each of powder pigments in Sienna yellow, Sienna red
and ochre brown
Half-litre barley white vinyl matt emulsion
Spray mount
Half-litre matt acrylic varnish

# BATHROOM FRESCO STENCIL
## *Step-by-step*
## *Stippled stencilling*

### *1.*

Transfer the two parts of Workpaper B to oiled stencil card (*see* page 78) and cut out the stencil with scalpel or scissors.

### *2.*

Dilute the barley white emulsion 50/50 with water in a container, and arrange the powder pigments separately on a plate.

### *3.*

Fix the stencil in place with spray mount (a light adhesive in an aerosol can). Pick up the dilute barley white on the tips of the brush bristles and then the Sienna yellow powder, wiping off the excess on newspaper before stippling through the stencil. Keep the brush at right angles to the wall. Continue in this way, using the Sienna red and ochre brown powders to shade and highlight. The stencil colours should be blended into the background as part of the painted wall, leaving gaps in the design to simulate wear.

*Transferring the design to the stencil card.*

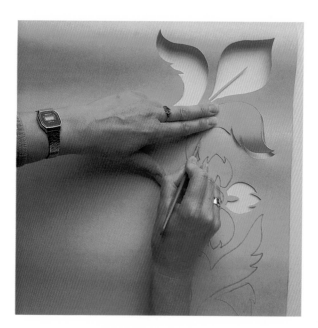

*Cutting out the design from the card with a scalpel.*

### 4.

As a finishing touch, stippled lines can be drawn around the stencil, painted between two pieces of masking tape.

### 5.

When dry, paint over the stencilled design with acrylic varnish.

*Using a stencil brush to apply the powder colours.*

*Masking off the area around the stencil to create lines.*

# DOORWAY STENCIL

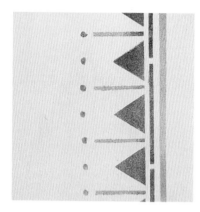

This simple design has been used round a doorway to link the colours of the rooms either side and to give more character to the plain door frame and skirting. Here the colours were sponged through the stencil to achieve a soft, not too strident effect, and the dots were later applied by hand in a slightly random manner, so as not to appear too strictly regimented.

# DECORATIVE MOTIFS AROUND THE HOME

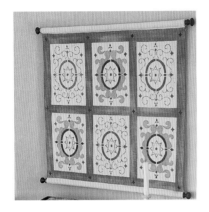

The plainest features of a home can easily be transformed in your own particular style using transferred or stencilled decorative motifs. These can be applied equally successfully on furniture, tiles or fabrics.

Having painted the marbled tiles of our Roman bathroom (*see* page 43), we turned our attention to painting a transferred design onto plain white tiles. We decided to frame twelve tiles to make a panel to decorate a kitchen wall, but the design is equally suited to unframed wall tiles in a bathroom or kitchen. We devised a simple, naive pattern, very loosely based on the sort of blue-and-white Delft patterns which would have been found in a typical Dutch kitchen. The tiles are quickly painted, particularly as any small errors add to the charm of an obviously hand-made design. Such faking of otherwise expensive painted tiles can be extended to all sorts of colours and designs: the bright patterns of Mexico or Portugal add a rustic, sunny touch to rooms; Victorian designs can be reproduced to complement the architecture of a house of the period. Museums, shops and magazines can all provide inspiration for the designs, or you could buy one wonderful, expensive tile to use as a template for the ones you paint yourself.

We then turned our decorative attention to fabric. If you have longed for a tapestry to hang on your wall but been deterred by the time and skill needed to sew one, our fake tapestry is the perfect alternative. Using paint which costs a fraction of tapestry wool, even a large tapestry can be produced very quickly.

Wallhangings are yet another interior design idea inherited from the past. As early as the fifteenth century, 'tapeters' were hung on interior walls to keep away damp and draughts in stone houses. In those days, itinerant painters would travel the country picking up commissions. They used egg tempera to colour their wallhangings - a mixture of egg yolk, linseed oil, water and powder colour. Many such wallhangings were designed to cover large areas, stretched between dado (chair rail) height and the ceiling, or hung loose in folds.

The wallhanging here can be completed in an afternoon. Once the stencil is cut it is a quick and simple task to stipple on the paint. The design could even be extended to make a very opulent bedspread, or be used on quick-to-finish table mats.

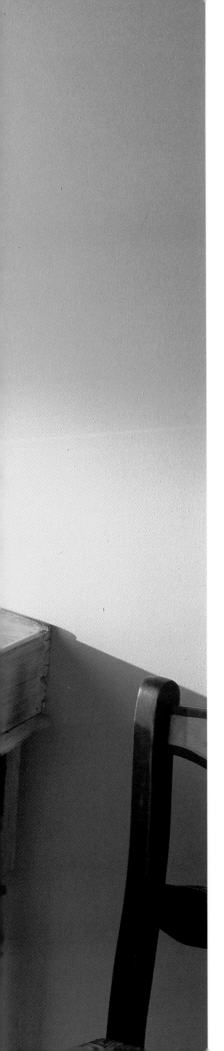

# A PATTERNED
# TILE PANEL

63

# A PATTERNED TILE PANEL
## *Step-by-step*
## *Distressing a frame*

### 1.

Mask off the plain tiles inside the frame with masking tape. Paint a smooth coat of off-white emulsion onto the bare frame. Allow to dry.

### 2.

Gently rub the wax candle around the edges of the frame and, working in one direction, on the flat part of the frame. Do not apply too much candle wax, as these areas are where the white will eventually show through to 'age' the frame.

*Painting the frame with off-white emulsion.*

*Rubbing a wax candle over the paint.*

### 3.

Completely paint the entire frame with dark blue emulsion and allow to dry.

### 4.

Using fine-grade wire-wool, gently rub the frame over in one direction until the off-white emulsion shows through on the waxed areas.

*Covering the wax with a coat of dark blue emulsion.*

*Rubbing the frame with wire-wool to reveal the off-white paint.*

# A PATTERNED TILE PANEL
## *Step-by-step*
## *Transfer painting on tiles*

### *1.*

Prepare the tiles by rubbing over the surface with wire-wool to roughen, and paint on a smooth, thin coat of tile primer with a wet brush. Allow to dry.

### *2.*

Transfer the two parts of Workpaper C to the areas of the tiles you wish to decorate, using carbon paper and pencil (*see* page 78).

### *3.*

Squeeze approximately ¹/₂-inch Prussian blue and of Titanium white acrylic colour spaced apart on a large plate. With the No 6 brush dipped in water, mix the blue and white together at the middle edges so that you have three shades of blue – dark, medium and light. The mid-blue will colour the border of the design, the pale blue the tree and birds and the dark blue and white will be used for high- and low-lighting detail.

*Transferring the design to the tiles using carbon paper.*

*Preparing the paints on a saucer.*

### 3.

Using the No. 6 brush, paint in the broader lines of the design. Aim for a brisk, painterly effect, in keeping with the naivety of the pattern.

### 4.

Using the No 3 brush, paint in the small details of birds' wings and swirls using dark blue and white.

### 5.

When dry, paint with two coats of polyurethane satin varnish.

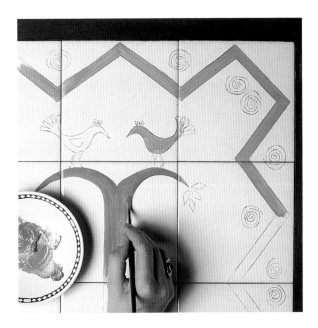

*Painting in the larger areas of the design.*

*Adding the finer details to the design.*

# A FAKE TAPESTRY

## SHOPPING LIST

Fabric cut to required size - heavy Indian cotton, hessian or
calico
Workpaper Designs D1 and D2
2 wooden dowel poles cut to horizontal fabric size
4 wooden or brass knobs to fit end of dowel poles
2B pencil
Stencil card
Scalpel or small, sharp scissors
Long ruler
Brown crayon
Small tins of vinyl matt emulsion in 3 colours: tawny red,
ochre yellow and dark blue
Stipple or stencil brush

# A FAKE TAPESTRY
### *Step-by-step*
### *Stencilling on fabric*

### *1.*

Transfer Workpapers D1 and D2 to stencil card and cut three stencils (*see* page 79). Workpaper D1 provides the stencil for panels stippled in tawny red, and Workpaper D2 two further stencils for panels to be painted respectively blue and ochre yellow (*see* steps 6. and 7.).

### *2.*

Using the brown crayon and ruler, mark in the rectangular panels of the design, spaced apart an inch and a half.

### *3.*

Paint in the borders by stippling tawny red emulsion onto the fabric. Keep the brush fairly dry, wiping excess paint off onto newspaper before applying to the fabric.

### *4.*

Using stencil D1, stipple in alternate panels with tawny red emulsion. Aim for a soft, fairly worn effect. Allow to dry.

### *5.*

Using the same stencil D1 and the tawny red emulsion, stipple in the remaining blank panels with only the central motif and the four little diamonds in the corners. Allow to dry.

*Drawing in borders and panels to edge the design.*

*Painting in the borders with tawny red emulsion.*

### 6.

Using the first stencil cut from D2 (black areas of the work-paper) and lining it up carefully over these second panels, stipple yellow ochre over the solid areas of the design.

### 7.

Using the second stencil cut from D2 (lined areas of the workpaper), stipple over with dark blue emulsion, taking care to line up the design. Allow to dry.

### 8.

Slot the dowel poles into seams at top and bottom of the hanging and attach knobs to ends.

*Using stencil D1 with the tawny red coloured paint in alternate panels.*

*Using the first stencil cut from D2 with yellow ochre paint around the central motif.*

*Adding dark blue to the same panels with the second stencil cut from D2.*

# Basic PREPARATION AND FINISHING TECHNIQUES

## Preparing walls

Basic preparation of walls is a boring but necessary evil, but there is no doubt that good preparation of the surface you intend to paint will pay dividends in the long term. 'Making good' the walls does have a calming effect. While you are washing down, filling and sanding, you also have time to consider the techniques and colours you intend to apply. You become aware of the faults and flaws in the wall which may need special care, and, in any case, there is no feeling as smug as that gained by achieving a smooth, expectant surface.

### Old (painted) plaster

Wash down the wall with a diluted solution of sugar soap dissolved in hot water. This will remove any flaking paint or plaster and reveal the small holes and cracks which need filling. Deep cracks should first be filled with all-purpose filler and then finished with a fine filler. First, rake out the crack to remove dust and loose plaster, then apply all-purpose filler. Allow plenty of time to dry and sand with medium-grade sandpaper. Top fill the crack with fine filler, and five minutes later smooth off excess with a damp sponge. Allow to dry thoroughly and then give a final sanding with wet-and-dry sandpaper. Apply two coats of your chosen base colour.

### New plaster

Always allow time for new plaster to completely dry out. Paint on a thin coat of sealer (a liquid solution which dries transparent and prevents any damp from seeping through the surface paint). When dry, paint with a thin coat of base colour, diluted with 10% water. When thoroughly dry, cover with one or two coats of base colour.

### WALLS IN VERY POOR CONDITION

If the walls are in very poor condition, you will obtain a much better paint finish if you line them first. Cracks should be filled as above, and the walls washed down with sugar soap. A coat of size (diluted wallpaper paste) brushed over the wall the day before you line is not essential, but will ensure an immaculate surface, free of bubbles or creases in the paper, on which to paint. After lining, allow the paper to dry out, then apply one coat of diluted (10%) base coat, before painting.

### PAPERED WALLS

It is not always necessary to remove old paper before painting. Washed down and lightly sanded, the old paper can serve as lining. Apply a first coat of diluted base paint before painting.

# PREPARING WOOD

### OLD WOOD IN REASONABLE CONDITION

Wash over doors and skirtings with a 70/30 solution of vinegar and water to neutralize any remaining grease. Remove any flaking paint and sand over lightly with medium-grade sandpaper. Any deep or unsightly cracks should first be painted with a small amount of wood primer or undercoat. Then fill the cracks with wood filler so that it stands proud. Smooth level with a damp sponge after about ten minutes. Allow to dry and sandpaper smooth.

If the paint technique you intend requires a very flat surface, you can paint the wood with two coats of acrylic gesso, sanding well in between. This works as a sealant and undercoat. Dilute wood primer is cheaper and can be used for the same purpose.

### NEW WOOD

Wood knots tend to occur more often in new wood. These should be sealed before painting, as paint will react with the wood resin and allow brown stains to seep through the finish. A patent 'knotting' solution can be purchased at most hardware stores. Two or three coats should be applied over the knots, each allowed to dry thoroughly. Sand the new wood lightly, apply a coat of wood primer, then paint.

## PREPARING TILES

First, rub over the tiles with wire-wool to imperceptibly break the surface glaze. Wash them with a 70/30 solution of vinegar and water to neutralize any remaining oil or grease. Allow to dry and paint over with tile primer, applied with a wet brush.

For a long-lasting finish and for tiles which need frequent cleaning, oil-based paints are toughest, and ceramic paint (epoxy enamel) is tougher still. The disadvantage of ceramic paint is that it is available only in a limited range of colours.

## FINISHING VARNISHES FOR WALLS

### POLYURETHANE

Most vinyl emulsion paints are tough enough to stand an occasional sponging down, but if your walls are subject to a lot of wear and tear, one or two coats of finishing varnish will give them good protection from knocks or steam. Polyurethane varnishes are suitable for use over most paint techniques and are made in three grades of shine - matt, satin and gloss. When buying, specify Clear Varnish, as some others will yellow with age and spoil the clarity of pale shades of paint.

Matt varnish is best suited to painting on rougher walls and over rustic paint effects, as it will not draw attention to imperfections. Satin varnish gives a pleasing sheen to a smooth paint technique. Gloss varnish is only appropriate if you want a very high shine, akin to Chinese laquer work. The solvent for polyurethane varnish is white spirit.

### ACRYLIC VARNISH

New on the market and available in the same finishes as polyurethane, acrylic varnishes are particularly suitable for use

over water-based wall paints, and have a quicker drying time. They do not yellow with age, but are a little harder to brush out smoothly than their oil-based counterparts. The solvent for acrylic varnish is water, making them a more environmentally friendly alternative.

### VARNISH BRUSHES

Any soft-bristled decorating brush is suitable. Choose the best you can afford and keep it specifically for use with varnish. A chisel-headed brush with graduated bristles cut straight across at the top will deliver the varnish a little at a time, producing a smooth, even coat.

'Gliders' are thin, light brushes for applying light varnishes which need a lot of brushing out. Their comparative expense is off-set by their ability to give the smoothest possible coat of varnish.

The best method of varnishing is to dip the brush into the varnish so that it is loaded half-way up the bristles. Wipe off any excess on the rim of the tin and paint in one direction for the first coat, across in the other for the second. This, with a little light sanding between coats, should eliminate any brush marks.

# USING THE WORKPAPERS

## TRANSFERRING
## A DESIGN

There are two simple methods for transferring a design from an existing illustration onto a wall or piece of furniture:

PENCIL If the workpaper does not fit precisely the area to be worked on, use a photocopier to reduce or enlarge it to the required size. Then simply scribble on the back of the designs with a soft (2B) pencil. Attach the paper, scribble side down, to the piece to be decorated, and then carefully draw over the outline of the design with a hard (HB) pencil. An impression of the soft pencil will trace the design on the piece, and any mistakes can be cleaned off with an eraser.

TRANSFER PAPER Place a piece of dressmaker's transfer paper onto the area to be decorated, and attach the workpaper over the top of it. Make both sheets firm with masking tape and then draw over the workpaper with a hard (HB) pencil.

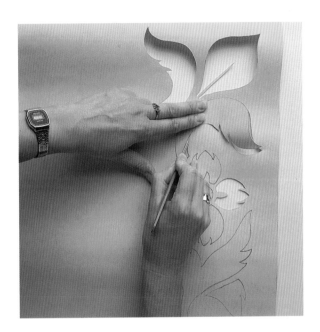

# CUTTING A STENCIL

You need a firm piece of card from which to cut your stencil. Manilla card coated with linseed oil is best as it is pliable, tough and easy to cut.

Transfer the workpaper design onto the card using either of the transfer methods outlined above. Place the stencil card onto a firm surface. Layers of newspaper on an old table work well, and are less expensive than an artist's cutting board. Use a lightweight, disposable scalpel for cutting out the design, and change the blade frequently.

Start cutting from the middle of the design, as this preserves the strength of the card; begin with the smaller details of the pattern; finish with larger areas. Draw the knife towards you, manoeuvering the card as you cut. The knife should be held at an angle of 45 degrees for a good, bevelled edge which will prevent paint from seeping beneath the stencil. Repair any mistakes made in cutting by sticking two small pieces of masking tape on either side of the card.

## BRIDGES

The bridges in a stencil are the linking pieces of card which
remain after cutting the design away. These links are important as
they hold the stencil together. The larger the areas of card which
are cut away, the larger the bridges should be to stabilize the stencil. Stencil bridges should recur at regular intervals and, if possible, be incorporated into the stencil design.

## EXTENDING A STENCIL

If you need to extend the pillars for our tracery wardrobe (*see*
page 50) to fit the door of your chosen piece, cut the pillars as
shown but leave linking pieces of card at approximately six inch
intervals from the base of the arch to the bottom of the pillar.